PRAYER BOOK

SAINT BARBARA

THE PROTECTOR AGAINST
LIGHTNING AND SUDDEN DEATH

Max Ivanova

Prayer Book Saint Barbara
"The Protector Against Lightning And Sudden Death "

Max Ivanova

First Edition/August 2022

Layout and cover design: Max Invanova.
Cover image "Saint Barbara" created by Max Ivanova.

Introduction

Dear reader, within the cosmos of religions and cults, we can find one of the greatest, the cult of Saint Barbara of Nicomedia. And there are countless people who claim to have received favors from such a singular martyr. To understand a little about the great power of Saint Barbara, we first need to get into the context of how she became the miraculous Saint we all know today.

Saint Barbara was born in Nicomedia, between the 3rd and 4th century, very close to the Sea of Marmara. Her father Dioscoro was a satrap (Persian governor) of strong character and somewhat cruel, so much so that he himself determines the confinement of his own daughter in a tower, to avoid the morbidity of men since Saint Barbara possessed an incomparable beauty. After the confinement of Santa Barbara in this tower she begins to enter into Christianity through reading, which would culminate in her total conversion to this religion.

At that time to profess such a religion in this place was considered a serious crime and therefore punishable by death. It is said that during Dioscoro's visit to another region, Bárbara takes advantage and orders to build three windows in the tower where she is imprisoned, all this as a direct allusion to the Holy Trinity, when her father returns and finds such construction he is surprised but it is not until later when he learns the meaning of the same, then he becomes enraged and wants to kill her with his own hands.

During the altercation Barbara barely manages to escape from her father and takes refuge in a rock, but later her father manages to recapture her after an intense search. Here a discrepancy arises because while some say that her father takes her to a court where she is tortured before being judged and finally killed in cold blood, others claim that it is at the top of this same rock where she is beheaded at the hands of her father and this is where the Divine vengeance arises, as it is said that at the moment in which he kills Saint Barbara with her own sword, a roar is heard in the sky and she is struck by lightning, which would end her life instantly. Saint Barbara appears with a crown in the form of a tower as an allusion to the confinement through which her conversion to Christianity took place, in her hand she holds a sword symbol of struggle and unwavering faith. Saint Barbara is associated with lightning and everything that has to do with explosives, that is why it is common to see her in some images with cannons in the background or artillery weapons.

Dear reader, in this book you will find some of the prayers and prayers most used by the devotees of Saint Barbara, all of them of incalculable spiritual value, if you are or intend to be initiated in the cult of Saint Barbara this book can not be missing in your collection, extend your knowledge and obtain peace and harmony in your life thanks to the intercession of Saint Barbara, patroness of lightning and sudden death, protect yourself and those you love the most, use the power of prayer to keep away from your life what you do not want.

4 December
Saint Barbara's Day

Prayer
Against Injustices
and Gossip

Oh, Blessed Saint Barbara!

You, who by the shedding of your
blood, offered chastity and
virginity to our Lord.

I (your name) ask you to defend
me from all injustice,
so that my life may always remain
pure and on the path of truth.

Oh, blessed Saint Barbara!

Do not allow my name
be on the lips of my detractors
keep away malicious remarks,
lies, slander.

Please always protect my
integrity, I beg you to cut with
your sharp sword those evil
tongues that at all costs want to
defame me.

Oh, Saint Barbara Martyr!

So great was your love for GOD
that you rejected your father's
all imposition, and he himself was
the cruel executioner
who had you beheaded.

Now that you live in glory
for ever and ever,
I (your name) humbly ask you to
intercede for me before our Lord.

For only in this way will I be able
to live my life in peace.

Oh Saint Barbara!

Help me to follow the path of goodness.

Deliver me from all evil, from envy, from evil eyes, from slander and all sorcery.

Oh, Blessed Saint Barbara!

With your conquering sword help me to drive away my enemies and all those who would do me harm.

Oh, Lord!

You who gave St. Barbara
incredible fortitude to endure the
greatest outrages and torments
out of fidelity to You.

I (your name) ask You that, like
her, I may be strong in adversity
and humble in prosperity
so that I may attain
eternal bliss.

Amen.

Prayer
To Saint Barbara
To Solve Problems
Of Love

Blessed Saint Barbara, glorious virgin!

Oh, just defender of the good!

You who received from Heaven strength in the face of the hardest adversity and who fought to preserve your faith, not to abandon the great love you have for GOD, make my eyes open towards Him, teach me to love Him at all times, renew my faith, my hope and rekindle in me the spirit of good deeds, give me a passionate devotion to GOD and open my heart towards those who suffer.

Oh, Virgin Saint Barbara!

Faithful martyr follower of Jesus, you who suffered to death for love, cast your merciful eyes upon me and grant relief to my sorrowful and sad heart.

You who were endowed with singular graces, today you enjoy great power in Heaven, hear my sincere prayer and grant me what I eagerly request, so that every beat and sigh of my afflicted heart, when they reach you, may become songs of joy and gladness.

Oh, Holy Virgin Barbara!

Relief for those who suffer, keep away the storms of my sentimental life, I need to find happiness and stop suffering.

Today I need to be with the person I love
(name of the person you love) please come to me and give me your help, make it possible to solve all the problems we have as soon as possible, drive away infidelity, jealousy and selfishness from our lives.

Oh, Saint Barbara!

effective advocate of ours, by the love you felt for Christ crucified, by your special power of intercession, by your great merits and many virtues, I beg you with all my heart, dear saint, attend to my sincere supplications of love, ask the Lord to help me to obtain what with all my hope I request of his goodness:

(mention the request).

Oh mighty righteousness of the impossible!

I ask you please to help me to fight in the defense of this great love that I feel today.

I also ask you, Blessed Saint Barbara, to give me your protection and protection, and to help me to live in my own flesh the transforming love of Jesus, to know how to apply his teachings and to live the fullness of the Spirit and enjoyment of GOD for all Eternity.

Amen.

Prayer
To Saint Barbara
To Increase Faith

Oh, Glorious Saint Barbara!

Faithful disciple of Jesus, You who resisted all the trials to which you were subjected to try to uproot your faith and yet you walked towards your martyrdom with great courage.

Help us to overcome all the trials to which we are subjected daily in our walk through this world, may we know how to give constant testimony of our faith.

Oh, Glorious Saint Barbara!

We want to remain faithful and
without anything or anyone
dragging us into evil.

Help me to pass these trials with
great faith and will.

Through Jesus Christ our Lord.

Amen.

Prayer
To Saint Barbara
To Solve
Love Problems

Oh, Saint Barbara!

Faithful relief of those who suffer, keep away the storms of my sentimental life, I need to find happiness and stop suffering, I need to be with the person I love; please come to me, give me your strength and help, make that as soon as possible we can solve all the problems we have, keep away infidelities, jealousy, selfishness, that a good relationship is established between us and we are united by solid bonds of love so that no one and nothing can separate us.

Oh, Saint Barbara!

Faithful advocate of ours, by the love you felt for Christ crucified, by your special power of intercession, by your great merits and many virtues, I (your name) beg you with all my heart, to attend to my sincere supplications of love, ask the Lord to help me to obtain it, today that with all my hope I request of his goodness:

(mention your request or love problem)

Oh, powerful warrior of the heavens!

Kind and compassionate Saint Barbara, I beg you to attend to the pleas of love that I have made to you, make sure that there are no obstacles between us, or people who wish to keep us apart, give us your assistance, do not delay in doing so, so that

(name the loved one)

be united to me in body and soul and we will never be separated.

Oh, Blessed Saint Barbara!

Make all impediments disappear, may all that distances us dissipate, may darkness give way to clarity so that we may reach the eternal light of union.

Protect us so that no one gets in the way of our relationship and that we may have a life full of harmony and love, perfect, full of understanding, full of happiness, rapport and harmony.

Oh, Holy Blessed Barbara!

Anoint my hair and quench my thirst with your infinite love.

Oh, mighty righteous one of the impossible!

Fight in defense of these eternal lovers. Grant that it may be so, that my desires may be fulfilled.

I also pray to you, blessed Saint Barbara, to give me your protection and protection.

Oh Holy Blessed One!

Give me understanding so that I may know how to apply his teachings, that I may live the fullness of the Spirit and enjoy GOD for all eternity.

Amen.

Daily Prayer To Saint Barbara

Oh, Most Glorious Virgin and
Martyr Saint Barbara!

Who for the ardent zeal for the
glory of GOD,
you suffered in a dark prison,
hunger, thirst and cruel scourging,
tolerating with patient admiration
that they tore to shreds
with burning tongs all your most
chaste and virginal body,
and your own Father took away
your life in order to go to fulfill
your first age in the Heavenly
Abodes.

We humbly beseech you
grant us a little of the grace of
Almighty GOD.

That we may succeed in serving
Him
by living in his holy fear
and suffering in this life with
patience
the tribulations that are offered to
us today.

So that when the terrible ordeal of
our last hour arrives,
may his Majesty grant us,
through his powerful intercession,
a true repentance of our faults.

May our consciences be purified in the salutary waters of the Sacrament and our souls nourished with the body and blood of Jesus in the Sacrament, and strengthened by the last anointing, may we enter triumphantly into the immense region of eternity and attain your company in Glory.
and attain your company in Glory.

Amen.

Prayer
To Saint Barbara
Against
Lightning

Oh, Blessed Saint Barbara!

That in heaven you are written
with paper and holy water.

Saint Barbara maiden,
deliver us from the lightning
and the ill-timed lightning.

Jesus Christ is nailed
on the altar of the Cross.

Our Father

Amen.

Prayer
Road Opener To
Saint Barbara

Oh, Holy Barbara!

Oh, Divine Power!

In times of trial,
I (thy name) humble and
unworthy creature, I beseech
Thee to help me to sustain myself
and not to fall into the wrong way.

Oh, Saint Barbara!

Lady of Lightning and storms....

I humbly ask You
to deliver me from the problems
that afflict me today.

Give me clarity of thought,
firmness and great strength.
Most holy martyr.

You who, locked in a tower
tower suffered because of your
father, so that men could not
admire your beauty, you were
converted and managed to escape
from your dark prison.

I beg you to unblock that which
what is holding me back today,
please break these material chains
that bind me:

For I am confident of your great
goodness and mercy
and I trust fully in the resolution
of my problems.

That is why, I (your name) offer
you this humble prayer.

I know that by means of your sword you will remove every obstacle from my path, with the force of the winds you will lift away from me every problem and impediment that today is stopping my progress.
and impediment that today is stopping my material as well as spiritual progress.
material as well as spiritual.

Oh, Saint Barbara!

Thank you for hearing my prayer.

Amen.

Prayer
To Ask for a
Favor
Urgent

Oh, Blessed Saint Barbara!

Oh, glorious Virgin, just defender of the good, you who received from Heaven strength in the face of the hardest adversity, you who fought to preserve the faith, not to abandon the great love you had for GOD, make my eyes open towards Him and teach me to love Him at all times, renew my faith, my hope and charity and revive in me the spirit of goodness, Please give me a passionate surrender to GOD and open my heart towards all those who suffer.

Holy Virgin Saint Barbara!

Martyr and faithful follower of
Jesus, you who suffered to death
for love, place your merciful eyes
on me and grant relief to this
painful and sad heart.

I ask you in the most humble way
to help me today in:
(mention your request)

So that I may have rest for my
tormented soul.

Holy Virgin Saint Barbara!

You who were endowed with singular graces, who enjoy great power in Heaven, hear my sincere prayer and grant me what I eagerly request of you, so that every beat and sigh of my afflicted heart, when they reach you, may become songs of joy and peace.

Amen.

Prayer
To free yourself
from any Storm

Oh, Holy Virgin Barbara!

Deliver us

Oh, blessed Saint Barbara
from all physical,
spiritual and moral
that may threaten our life today,

Blessed Saint!

Protect us and watch over us.
Deliver us from lightning, from
the winds of storms and
hurricanes, from misfortunes and
dangers.

Oh, Blessed Saint Barbara!

Protect our homes
and our properties, from the
accidents that bad weather may
cause.

Protect us also, dear Saint
Barbara, from the dangers that
threaten our faith,
from the abandonment of
religious practice and from
indifference to our brothers and
sisters who need our help today.
who today need our help.

Oh, Blessed Saint Barbara!

Give us strength for those difficult days we still have to go through so that one day we may enjoy the happiness of Heaven.

Amen.

Novena To
Saint Barbara

Day I

GOD of mercy, merciful GOD,
clement GOD,
You who gave to the Glorious
Virgin and Martyr Saint Barbara,
light, knowledge and admirable
discretion to venerate the Most
High Mystery of the august and
ineffable Holy Trinity
of the august and ineffable Holy
Trinity, firmly believing and
adoring with greater constancy
the unity of the essences and the
trinity of the persons:

We humbly beg you to grant us
through their merits and
intercession
that they always remained
steadfast in this Holy Faith and
belief,
may we merit to die confessing so
high a mystery
through Jesus Christ Our Lord,
who with you and the Holy Spirit,
lives and reigns for ever and ever.

Amen.

(Make The Petition)

Pray for us, Blessed Saint Barbara
to the Divine Majesty:

That we may be free from sudden
death!

Most Glorious Virgin and Martyr
Saint Barbara!

Patroness and my advocate:
come to my aid in the last days of
my life,
so that through your intercession
I do not die without the help of
the Holy Sacraments,
but that before my soul separates
from this body, I may obtain
from Thy Heavenly spouse
true and entire contrition and
sorrowful confession,
Holy Communion and the last
anointing, and may I pass from
this exile to accompany You in
Eternal Glory.

Amen.

Day II

Oh Almighty GOD and Lord
Almighty!

You alone endowed the Blessed
Virgin and Martyr
Saint Barbara with such fortitude
to suffer the most cruel torments
in defense of the august mystery
of the august mystery of Your
incomprehensible Trinity:

"dispose of our hearts
by her merits and powerful
intercession".

So that from this moment on, under the protection of divine grace, may we resist with courage and constancy to all the snares of our capital enemies; Lord grant that, strengthened with faith, encouraged with hope and inflamed with charity; may we embrace the Divine inspirations, may we fulfill in everything and for everything your Most Holy will, and may we attain in this life the favor we ask for in this novena; may we praise You for eternities in Glory.

Amen.

Day III

Oh GOD and Lord of infinite goodness!

You alone instilled in the Glorious Virgin and Martyr Saint Barbara the most ardent desires to enlist under the banners of Jesus Christ through the Sacred Baptism to enlist under the banners of Jesus Christ by means of Sacred Baptism, with whose sacrosanct waters I extinguish for ever the ardors of Concupiscence; Lord, grant that through her merits and powerful intercession

May the Spiritual sprinkling of
Divine Grace extinguish the
voracious fire of our faults,
so that, clothed once again
with the stole of Grace
may we merit, together with the
special favor that we ask of you in
this holy novena, to live and die
in a holy way and to make us
participants in the last day of our
life of that eternal Blessing which
you have reserved for the elect, in
whose company we shall praise
you in Glory.

Amen

Day IV

Oh GOD and Lord of eternal
majesty!

Who among the hard stones
granted a safe asylum to the
Glorious Virgin and Martyr Saint
Barbara when fleeing from the
rigor of her implacable Father,
a rock miraculously opened up to
give her free passage:

We humbly beseech Thee, O Lord, that by His merits and intercessions soften the hardness of our hearts, so that by bearing fruits worthy of penance, we imitate the heroic virtues of our Patroness and advocate. and advocate.

And so let us occupy ourselves unceasingly in the meditation of Thy ineffable mysteries, may we obtain the favor we humbly request in this novena.

We praise You for eternities in Glory.

Amen.

Day V

Oh, GOD and Lord of incomprehensible wisdom!

You who witnessed how the Glorious Virgin and Martyr Saint Barbara was stripped naked by tyrannical and sacrilegious hands and covering all her virginal body with the precious purple of her shed Blood

to the impulse of cruel scourging,
so that they might imitate in some
way the sufferings of your most
beloved Son.

Lord, through his merits and
powerful intercession, may we
strip ourselves of the sinful habits
that daily drag us to evil,
clothe us with the Cross of
mortification
so that we may thus attain Thy
infinite mercy and pity,
as well as the favor we ask in this
Novena.

Oh, Merciful Lord!

Give us an innocent life and a death like that of the Righteous One
to praise You for Eternities in Glory.

Amen.

(Make the petition)

Day VI

Oh, GOD and Lord Omnipotent!

Glory of the martyrs, joy of the just and splendor of the angels.

You who gave to the Glorious Virgin and Martyr Saint Barbara so much serenity and impavor to see her beautiful lips embraced with flaming axes, her head tormented with cruel blows with cruel blows and wounded her pious ears

with so many insults and
blasphemies,
We humbly beseech Thee, O
Lord, by her merits and
intercession, to kindle in our
hearts the flame of Thy divine
Love, so that we may constantly
offer Thee all the labors and
hardships of this life.

All of them united with those of
our Protectress so that we may
obtain Your sovereign clemency
and the favor we ask for in this
Holy Novena.

the participation in the Holy
Sacraments
and the possession of eternal bliss.
Amen.

(Make the petition)

Day VII

Oh, GOD Lord Admirable in all
Thy works!

Thou who didst witness how Saint
Barbara was
exposed to shame
in the streets and squares of
Nicodemus, led naked to the
courts in the sight of such
sacrilegious eyes, You covered her
whole body with a garment of
snow as resplendent as the sun.

Oh, Holy Lord!

We beseech You to grant us
through their merits and
intercession that at the hour of
death,
when our souls are exposed to the
vituperation
of our enemies, may you cover us
with the most pure snow
of Jesus in the Blessed Sacrament,
serving us as food and food for
the painful journey to Eternity.

Lord, deliver us from the confusion and shame of guilt and grant us the favor we ask of You in this humble novena.

Amen.

(Make the petition)

Day VIII

Oh, GOD and Lord of Great Clemency!

Consolation of the afflicted and refuge of the troubled, who didst grant to the Glorious and Virgin Saint Barbara special graces and favors to dispense to all her devotees;

Especially in storms, tempests, earthquakes and sudden deaths, we beseech Thee to grant us, by their merits and powerful intercession, that when Thy justice against our faults is irritated, Thou wilt not strike us with these terrible scourges. with these terrible scourges of Thy wrath, Oh Lord.

We ask You to remember the Sacred Iris of Peace, which You have placed on the horizons of our world and have mercy on its faithful and devoted devotees...

Oh, Holy Lord!

Exhort us to a true penance, so
that with the recognition of our
misery, we may even attain in this
life the favor
in this life the favor we ask for in
this Holy Novena, a blessed death
and Eternal Glory.

Amen.

Day IX

Oh, GOD and Lord of all virtues!

Thou who didst enrich the
Glorious Virgin and Martyr Saint
Barbara with a special power to
protect her faithful devotees
in the agonies of death,
especially so that they may not
pass into eternity
without receiving the Sacraments,

as countless sinners have
experienced;

We earnestly beseech Thee, by his
merits and powerful intercession,
to incline Thy most pious ears to
hear the Your most pious ears to
listen to the supplications
which we have addressed to Thee
in this Holy Novena:

We beseech Thee to grant us the
special favor
which we have so longingly asked
of Thee on this day;

Lord, grant us at last all the help
we need to partake of the
to partake of the Holy
Sacraments,
to die in eternal peace and to bless
you eternally in Glory.

Amen.

Note: This powerful novena has to be done for 9 days in a row at the same time, you can light a white candle before starting the prayer and at the end let the candle burn completely and pray three Our Fathers and a Hail Mary.

Prayer
To Saint Barbara
Against Envy and
Enemies

Oh, Saint Barbara!

Chaste maiden and glorious martyr, faithful witness of Jesus Christ until your death, who by following his Word and not losing faith, with the palm of martyrdom and crown of flowers you are in Glory with GOD the Son and his Blessed Mother: give us today your protection on this day and on all occasions.

Guide us along the best paths, keep away from us all evil spirits as well as my enemies, and bring to my life, well-being, peace and love.

Oh, Holy Blessed Barbara!

From the immense throne where you are already happy, hear us!

Since with fervor we ask for a little of your attention, attend us with mercy, since today I require more than ever your holy protection.

Blessed Saint Barbara!

You who in Heaven are written with paper and holy water, keep the bread, keep the wine and the people on the road.

Holy Barbara maiden, who in heaven are now a star, deliver us from all evil, lightning and sparks!

Jesus Christ is nailed to the tree of the Cross. Our Father Amen Jesus.

Barbara, holy and glorious!

Warrior of the heavens, powerful intercessor before the Lord, you who act as defender and protector, receive me today, for your favor I come to implore.

Saint Barbara, blessed virgin and martyr, great and of immense power, GOD be with you, GOD enlighten you and you me, in every bad moment, in every occasion, lead me always on the path of good.

Oh, Saint Barbara!

With your conquering sword deliver me from evil, from injustice, from envy and rancor, from evil leagues, gossip, gossip and defamation, from treason, from intrigues and evil eyes.

With the power of lightning keep me away from evil people, protect me from my enemies, visible or invisible, known or unknown, and deliver me from everything that can cause me harm, keep me away from betrayal, hatred, jealousy and resentment, and let me always be victorious in any bad situation, incident or danger.

With the chalice of your cup and wine maintain the strength of my body and spirit for the hard struggle and combat of life.

Oh, Saint Barbara!

Please attend to my supplications and prayers and to the flowers that I give you, receive them as an offering that I have you always present in my thoughts and in my home, and I beg you to never abandon me and to come to me every time I ask you to defend my faith, my life and that of my loved ones, my loves, my family and my struggles; and that in the end you take me to the Glory where you now enjoy Eternity!

Saint Barbara, to your protection I entrust myself, make God hear me in this my petition:

(Make the petition)

May your protection and help always accompany me, may your love and fidelity to Christ serve me as an example, and may your strength and tenacity help me to be better each day, so that I may be able to live in holy friendship and reach the end of my days with great peace in His Divine Grace.

Amen.

Prayer
To Saint Barbara
To Recover A Love

Oh, Glorious martyr Saint
Barbara!

Faithful disciple of Jesus,
of virtuous soul and firm heart in
your beliefs,
You who withstood all the trials to
which they subjected you
to try to wrest from you your
faith in Our Lord.

You who walked towards
martyrdom with joy and courage,
because of the love you felt for
Christ, our Savior.

Saint Barbara, blessed virgin!

Saint of immense splendor,
today with affection we come to
you asking you to assist us and
help us
and help us to overcome all these
trials and difficulties
to which we are subjected
in our hard walk through this
world,
may we know how to give
constant witness to our faith
as you did in spite of adversity.

We want to remain firm and faithful, without anything or anyone dragging us down to evil, and to pass through any trial with hope and faith on high. trusting always as you do in Divine Providence.

Oh, Saint Barbara!

You who give us help, pray for us, give us your prodigious help and protection, for the purity and goodness that you have in your soul.

Please do not abandon us
in bad situations,
help us when we are in despair,
and plead for us before the Most
High when distress and affliction
oppress us.

Holy One full of power, Blessed
Saint!

You who are most efficacious
advocate in loving affairs
and soothe our heart when it
suffers and groans in pain,
pray for us before the throne of
the Eternal Father.

So that my sentimental life may
be fixed, so that I may regain my
joy and the desire to live
and that I may be with the person
with whom I am in love,
(name the loved one)
with a true, faithful, sincere and
reciprocated love.

Please take away everything that
prevents us from being happy,
may nothing separate me from
the person I love!

May no one interfere or want to
break our relationship
so that we may live together,
devoted and happy.

Grant us, Oh Holy Warrior!

That we may be united again,
that we may be a couple, a stable
marriage, so that both of us may
live a beautiful and sweet love
story.

Oh, Saint Barbara!

I pray to you for me, so that I may
obtain solution
in the difficulties and serious love
problems
that do not allow me to be with
the person that I love so much
and that I wish so much to have
by my side night and day:

(Make the petition)

Oh, Blessed Saint Barbara!

Only in you I trust, to you I cry out in my pain, because you know how much I need to be heard, I leave everything in your miraculous hands, I know that you will intercede for me before GOD Almighty.
I know that you will intercede for me before the Almighty GOD and you will obtain for me the help that I sincerely request.
So be it.

Amen.

Prayer
To Saint Barbara
Against Dispossession
and Seizure

Blessed Saint Barbara!

Beauty and martyrdom together, with your sword I persecute myself and because of your infinite goodness I embrace your justice.

Blessed Saint Barbara!

That in heaven you are written with paper and holy water, free the bread, free the wine, free the people from danger, free me from injustice, protect my roof, my clothes and my sustenance.

Oh, Blessed Saint Barbara!

You who are written in the sky, in the valley the sands, in the sky the stars, guard my belongings from the evil usurer, do not allow me to be a victim of the cursed robbery.

Blessed Saint Barbara!

I ask you that the house where I live, which is my property, be free by your sword of all judicial process, that there be no fees or embargoes and that they cannot take it away from me.

Do not allow the usurer to evict me from my home, for I am a poor worker and it is my blessed property, the fruit of my work and sweat, and if I was late in making payments, it was because I could not provide for the support of my family, and I had many difficulties and I was desperate.

Oh, Blessed Saint Barbara!

You who are written in heaven with paper and holy water, may your sword protect me and act against injustice.

Allow me to keep my property for
your greater glory, for I am your
faithful devotee and with humility
I shelter under your protection
and protection.

Amen

Prayer
To Saint Barbara
To Ask Her
Her Protection

Oh, glorious and blessed Saint Barbara!

Martyr of Christ who was subjected to hard trials and, without ever losing courage, firmness and courage you fought in the good fight of the Lord, and became strong against the most terrible tortures to preserve your faith and virginal purity, you who now joyfully occupy a privileged place in Heaven and are the joy of the Eternal Father and of the Blessed Virgin, of the Angels and Saints, remember your faithful devotees....

that we are still battling in the hard struggles of life surrounded by enemies, dangers and needs and give us great Saint, your patronage, help and protection.

Oh, Saint Barbara!

Full of immense strength and power, we come to pay you heartfelt homage and praise, and to beg you to intercede for us now and always, for we know that the Lord promised you that He would not deny anything to anyone who asked for it through the merits of your martyrdom and precious death,

That is why we pray to you:

May you keep us away from
winds, lightning and storms,
deliver us from magics, sorceries
and sudden death, confuse and
keep away from us our enemies
and bad people, help to solve our
problems of love, defend us with
your sword from evil eyes and
wickedness, from injustices, envy,
defamations and evil tongues
from evil eyes and wickedness,
from injustice, envy, slander and
evil tongues, deliver us from jails
and prisons, guide us on the roads
eliminating obstacles and attract
prosperity and abundance to our
lives.

Especially, Holy benefactress, attend to this supplication that I make to you with all my faith and hope:

(Make the petition)

You who by the mercy and goodness of our GOD in the misfortunes and sufferings you endured received divine assistance, ask also for us help in our afflictions and obtain for us from the infinite majesty of the Lord, what we have confidently asked for in this prayer.

Oh, Blessed Saint Barbara!

Grant us constant protection against all dangers of body and soul, and obtain for us the grace of a true and sincere love for our adorable Savior Jesus Christ, to whom be all honor and glory forever and ever.

Amen.

Oración
To Saint Barbara
To Recover Your
Couple Quickly

Oh, Blessed Saint Barbara!

You who are the beloved daughter of GOD and who offered yourself in sacrifice to the Creator of heaven, for you preferred martyrdom and death rather than renounce the eternity of your soul.

You who are an advocate against the harshest inclemencies, today in my painful and sad present I come to you with fervor and hope to ask you to heal my heart and bring me back to my absent love.

Oh, Blessed Saint Barbara!

Do not allow this family disunity, make us solve and resolve as soon as possible the problems and differences in our relationship.

You who work so many miracles and believe in love, make possible the return of:

(name the loved one)

with hope and do not allow anyone to interfere in our union,

Remove from us every person, obstacle and temptation so that with respect, forgiveness and understanding we may move forward together in the fullness of love and that the sun may shine again in my tormented heart.

Oh, Saint Barbara!

Dispel all doubts and emotional storms, which were the cause of separation and unite our family again in happiness, love and peace, restore calm and good times between us.

Without reproaches, without problems, without displeasure, do it for us, so that together and in harmony we may advance.

You who with Divine justice wear the crown of light that you won on this earth thanks to merit and virtue, listen to my anguished petition and take it before our GOD and Lord so that by his mercy and goodness it may be granted, I will do everything in my power to preserve the happiness that through your mediation I obtain, and I promise you devotion for the rest of my life.

Blessed Saint Barbara!

I ask you also to help me to love the Lord as you loved him, and the joy of living and dying in his friendship and grace, to see him, love him, enjoy him and glorify him in your company for ever and ever.

Warrior of the heavens Blessed Saint Barbara!

Please attend to my supplications of love so that I and my love may be united in body and soul.

Protect us so that no one may stand in the way of our paths of happiness and union.

Anoint my hair and quench my thirst with your infinite love for my good desires.

Mighty righteous one of the impossible, fight in defense of these eternal lovers.

Saint Barbara, glorious virgin and martyr!

May we become united again and live together in peace, love and loyalty.

I never stop thinking about

(name the person I love)

and I know that I want to spend the rest of my life by his or her side, for I think we are destined to live a future together,

With all my soul I wish that we will be together again to love each other properly.

I want him to give himself body and soul to me; I ask for your mediation to recover the happiness we had, that the mistakes and errors be forgiven and forgotten, that the obstacles and barriers be removed and any person who wants to separate us disappear, so that the love that still beats in our hearts may triumph.

Oh, Lord Almighty!

I beg you, Lord, through the merits of your dear Saint Barbara, whom your omnipotence strengthened, your wisdom enlightened and your love inflamed, grant me strength, help and health, in these moments of distress.

Saint Barbara, you are stronger than the tower of a fortress and the fury of hurricanes.

Let not the lightning strike me, the thunder frighten me or the roar of cannons shake my courage or strength.

Be always by my side so that I may face all the storms and battles of my life with my head held high and my face serene.

For I want to win every fight, and I am conscious of doing my duty, I thank you, my protector, and I surrender to GOD, Creator of heaven, earth and nature, who has the power to subdue the fury of the storm and mitigate the cruelty of war.

Oh, Blessed Santa Barbara!

Venerated in East and West for the great faith that I place in you And because of the hope that you inspire in me, I trust that you will raise my prayers to Heaven and that from GOD and the Virgin they will send me urgent help and my life will once again be full of joy and happiness.

I trust in your strength and your great power, I trust in your gracious protection and your effective mediation and I thank you from the depths of my being, for you will never again allow us to be separated.

Take my petitions as soon as possible to GOD and the Virgin Mary, ask them for blessings and help in my difficult situation and that they fill my life with faith and charity towards others so that I may deserve to participate in the glory that you enjoy in Heaven.

Blessed Virgin Mary, mother and consolation of those who suffer, I beg you, in all humility, hear this prayer, dedicated to blessed Saint Barbara.

I (your name) promise you to amend my faults, I beg you to allow Saint Barbara to free me from this evil that I suffer and that is my martyrdom and suffering.

From the depths of my being I beg you not to leave me without an answer,

Help me to fulfill my dreams so that we may move forward together in harmony.

Oh, Saint Barbara!

You alone are my refuge and my comfort, my hope and my encouragement, please be my mediator before the Most High so that He may extend His merciful hand to me.

Amen.

Prayer
To Saint Barbara
To Attract
Money And
Abundance

Oh, Beloved Saint Barbara!

Great Lady of lightning and thunder, owner of all gold and silver.

I thank you for all the favors obtained.

I thank you for the health that keeps me on my feet, for the family you have granted me and for the love I receive from heaven.

I also thank you for the wisdom that is given to me daily thanks to your Grace.

Oh, Beloved Saint Barbara!

I thank you for the food on my table, for I acknowledge your support in the name of GOD.

Continue to bless me, Mother, and open the doors of prosperity so that I may live happily and carefree.

Multiply in my life gold and silver, as well as health, work and love.

Not because I deserve it, but because I know that you will never abandon us to our fate.

Saint Barbara, true and strong faithful saint of those who need your help and protection.

Oh, Beloved Saint Barbara!

Today I ask you with much faith to give me your help urgently in my financial life as it is getting worse every day.

That is why I ask you to help me to earn and manage my income better.

So that I don't go through these financial difficulties anymore.

I need to bring more abundance into my life and the lives of the people I love so much,

Give me the opportunity to find a decent and well paid job to have a better quality of life.

Thank you beloved mother for hearing my pleas and not leaving me alone in this painful situation.

Amen.

Prayer
To Saint Barbara
To Pray For The
Health Of A Sick
Person

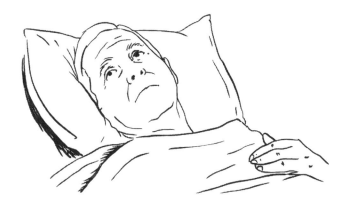

Oh, my beloved Saint Barbara!

I adore and admire you, for my heart is always ready to serve you.

I thank you with all my heart for having offered your life in exchange for your Faith.

Today, I (your name) come to you to ask for the healing of a soul devoted to you, who is going through unfortunate times.

(Say the name of the sick person)

Have mercy and grant that these hours may be free from torture and deliver me from future health problems through your holy will.

For I know that you are a source of mercy and consolation, a faithful protector of souls in an unfavorable situation.

Today with deep faith I turn to you, with total conviction, grant me and all the affected family members the strength we need.

Repress the fatality in my life and in the lives of those around me who are suffering today because of this affliction.

Oh, Saint Barbara!

Restore the health of:

(name the sick person)

For no one like you has the mettle, the power and the spiritual strength to perform this miracle.

I ask that all mortality that wants to destroy him/her this day, may You remove it from his/her body and eradicate it completely.

Heal him/her of all ailments and deliver him/her from the hour of distress!

Oh, Blessed Saint Barbara!

Intercede for:

(Name the sick person)

That his sins may be forgiven as well as his faults and errors, since we know that they are the consequence of this illness manifesting itself in his life.

Cover us with your mantle, dear Mother, so that we may be immune to all evil.

As well as any disease that threatens any member of my family.

We trust in your immense power, blessing and protection.

Thank you for interceding before Almighty GOD and imploring Him for our healing.

Oh, Beloved Saint Barbara
Blessed!

We love you.

Amen.

Prayer
To Saint Barbara
To Get The Love Of A
Person

Oh, Most glorious virgin and martyr Saint Barbara!

You who reached the Kingdom of Heaven, strong warrior who never lost your courage, even in the face of the most terrible tortures, you who give help to those who suffer for love, I want to ask you to make use of your great power and intercede for me, because I need your help to solve my afflictions.

Oh, Blessed Saint Barbara!

Effective advocate of ours, my
friend, confidant and special
protector, I deposit in you all my
hopes, I know that I will not be
disappointed because you are the
most generous.

I beg you to take my supplications
to GOD and beg him to grant me
as soon as possible to obtain what
I desire so much:

Well, I love:

(name the loved one)

with all my heart and I want to get his or her love, I want him or her to love me body and soul forever, I want to share my life with him or her and let nothing and no one stand in our way.

Please remove every obstacle that prevents our union, make him think of me, make him value me, make his heartbeat unite with mine, make him only want to be with me and make him realize that I feel an intense and true love for him, so that we can be a happy couple, a couple where love, respect and peace reign, and become one thought and one being.

Oh, Saint Barbara!

You who always attend to those who come to you, I know that you will have pity on me and give me your powerful help.

From the depths of my being I beg you not to leave me without an answer, make my dreams come true of being the only love of:

(name the loved one)
so that we may move forward together in harmony.

Saint Barbara, you alone are my refuge and my consolation, my hope and my encouragement, the mediator for me before the Most High.

I pray also that you may be my strength in the face of adversity and that I may always be attentive to those who need my help, for only in this way will I be able to reach the end of my days in peace with your Divine Glory.

Amen.

The 2 Hour Prayer To Come Back And Never Go Away

Oh, Saint Barbara!

Prodigious Celestial Warrior!

Today I come to you with humility, faith and great trust, to ask you for this urgent favor, given the circumstances that have occurred in my life and the impossibility of remedying them.

Today I have recourse to you, Holy Barbara since you never abandon me and you never fail me, because you always listen to me and attend to all my needs.

Oh, Blessed Saint Barbara!

Justiciar of the impossible!

Make (name the loved one) think of me, remember me, that my name is repeated over and over again in his mind and that he feels every minute my absence as a prick in his heart, that he can no longer wait a second to call me and hear my voice.

Make me desperately seek any means to do so.

Oh, Blessed Saint Barbara!

Protector of lovers, make him/her: (name the loved one) come to me with longing and desire for me, kneeling and begging for my affection and love.

Oh, Blessed Saint Barbara!

You who are the defender of eternal lovers, anoint the heart of:
(name the loved one)
so that he/she may value this love that I feel and thus give me a privileged place in his/her life.

So that he/she will have the courage to face any obstacle or person that comes between us.

Oh, Holy Barbara warrior of the heavens!

Unite our souls and our hearts with the bonds of eternal love, with the strength of the love of GOD the Father.

With the sweetness of the heart of the Blessed Virgin Mary, powerful guardian of Divine justice, return to:

(name the loved one)
to my life forever.

May he never turn away and never stop loving me, may he never have doubts, may fear never invade him and may he always fight and defend our great love!

Amen.

Note: This powerful prayer has to be done for 7 days in a row at the same time, you can light a red candle before starting the prayer and at the end let the candle burn out.

Prayer to Saint Barbara for Difficult Cases

Oh, Saint Barbara!

Advocate and intercessor of those who suffer, take with humility and with the same love that you receive in heaven, this humble supplication and this prayer.

For today I present to you this impossible case:

(Make the petition)

And it is for me an obligation and an urgent necessity to obtain from you the solution that I desire so much.

Since a favorable answer will give peace to my soul, dear Saint Barbara, you know that human frailty and incapacity prevent us from acting on our own, therefore we have recourse to your power and glory and to heavenly grace.

Oh, Glorious Saint Barbara!

You who are on the Holy Land have already embraced the Divinity!

It is for this reason that I (your name) ask you to fill with your presence my needs, my misfortunes and my intentions that you already know, because I know that in heaven where you are, nothing is denied to you.

Today I am faced with a case that is almost impossible for me, from which my human strength is insufficient, please intercede for me, you who by your grace nothing is denied to you!

Pray with perseverance for:

(Make the petition)

I do not even want to think what will become of me if I do not obtain your holy favors!

I know that thanks to your holiness, you will make our Holy Father come soon to grant and help me in my need.

And above all I know that my case, left in your hands, will not go unanswered!

Saint Barbara, source of countless graces and blessings, for having conquered the heavenly altars, intercede and pray for us and protect us from all evil and injustice!

Oh, mighty and humble Lady!

Intercede for us before our Blessed Father!

So that He may deign to grant me this urgent favor and place on my side the victory and the solution to my problems, thanks to the power of heaven.

May Your protection embrace my humanity and may Your Holiness permeate my intentions, and for Your sake may the Great Power of Heaven tip the scales always in my favor!

Oh, Saint Barbara!

May the abundance in the Father's heart be poured out upon my need and may the grace which you enjoy in heaven extend to where I am and not only cover my fragile and human being but also reach beyond where my human capacities do not reach.

So that with brevity and according to the will of the Father my case may reach heavenly favors.

Thank you for having listened to me, noble and beloved Saint Barbara, I wait anxiously for the good news.

Amen.

Dear readers, we have reached the end of this book but first I would like to tell you that in this subject of prayers and prayer, faith plays a fundamental role, this has been a small but powerful fragment of a whole world of prayers that have been dedicated to Saint Barbara, I hope you have enjoyed it as much as I have enjoyed writing it for you, I am Max Ivanova and I wish that your greatest desires become an absolute reality, until next time!

The End

Made in the USA
Columbia, SC
15 December 2023

d00ed922-d5b5-4a94-8a7c-5d7e8c0fb5eeR01